# zoom español 1

## Higher Workbook

Vincent Everett

OxBox

OXFORD

Great Clarendon Street, Oxford OX2 6DP

Oxford University Press is a department of the
University of Oxford.

It furthers the University's objective of excellence in research, scholarship,
and education by publishing worldwide in
Oxford  New York  Auckland  Cape Town  Dar es Salaam  Hong Kong  Karachi
Kuala Lumpur  Madrid  Melbourne  Mexico City  Nairobi  New Delhi  Shanghai
Taipei  Toronto

With offices in
Argentina  Austria  Brazil  Chile  Czech Republic  France  Greece  Guatemala
Hungary  Italy  Japan  South Korea  Poland  Portugal  Singapore  Switzerland
Thailand  Turkey  Ukraine  Vietnam

British Library Cataloguing in Publication Data

Data available

ISBN 978 019 912756 6

20 19 18 17 16

Printed in Great Britain by Ashford Colour Press Ltd.

**Acknowledgements**

The Publisher and authors would like to thank the following for their permission to
reproduce photographs and other copyright material:

Cover: Oxford Designers & Illustrators

P46: Brendan Howard/Shutterstock.

Illustrations by: Adrian Barclay, Stefan Chabluk. Theresa Tibbetts, James Stayte.

Audio recordings: Colette Thomson for Footstep Productions,
Andrew Garratt (Engineer)

# Tabla de materias

# Pronunciation

## Vowels

**1** 🎧 Listen and practise the vowels with the actions.

**2** 🎧 Practise saying the names of these Spanish football clubs. Listen and check.

> Gran Canaria  Salamanca  La Palma  Osasuna  Granada

**3** 🎧 Try these combinations of vowels. Say them separately, then together, then in a word. Listen and check.

> | | | |
> |---|---|---|
> | u – a | ua | cuatro |
> | e – i | ei | seis |
> | e – i | ei | veinte |
> | i – e | ie | siete |
> | u – e | ue | nueve |

**4** Now try saying these Spanish football clubs.

> Real Oviedo  Bilbao  Santiago  Eibar  Huelva

**5** Remember to pronounce all the vowels. Say these words.

> siete  nueve  once  doce  quince

**6** Say these Spanish football clubs.

> Levante  Tenerife  Elche

# Pronunciation

## Soft and hard consonants

**1** 🎧 Listen and repeat these words. Underline the soft c
(pronounced like 'th').

> casa   cinco   cocina

**2** 🎧 Listen and repeat these words. Underline the soft g / j
(pronounced like 'ch' in 'loch').

> geografía   Los Ángeles   José

**3** 🎧 Find the soft ci / ce / z sound and underline it in these Spanish football
clubs. Say the words, then listen and check.

> Barcelona   Albacete   Celta de Vigo   Zaragoza

**4** 🎧 Find the soft ge / gi / j sound and underline it in these Spanish football
clubs. Say the words, then listen and check.

> Gijón   Getafe   Ejido

**5** Use everything you've learned so far. Underline the tricky bits in these
words, then try saying them.

> Badajoz   Jerez   Real Murcia   Córdoba   Numancia de Soria

# Pronunciation

## Spanish consonants

**1** 🎧 **Listen, then practise saying these sounds. First on their own, then in words.**

| | | |
|---|---|---|
| qu | qu | ¿qué? |
| ll | ll | me llamo |
| rr | rr | burro |
| ch | ch | ocho |
| ñ | ñ | España |

**2** 🎧 **Listen carefully to the words. Circle the correct answer.**

What happens to the letter v? *Same as English / hard to tell / a bit like a 'b'.*

What happens to the letter d? *Same as English / hard to tell / a bit like a 'th'.*

voy   verde   identidad   ciudad

**3** **In *er*, *ir* and *ar*, do not change the sound of the vowel from 'e', 'i' or 'a'. Try saying these words.**

verde   número   ir al baño   escuchar

**4** **Underline the tricky consonants, then try saying the names of these Spanish football clubs.**

Real Valladolid   Deportivo La Coruña   Español   Mallorca
Valencia   Villarreal   Sevilla   Rayo Vallecano
Atlético Madrid   Real Sociedad   Santander   Almería   Tenerife

**5** **Pretend to read the Spanish football results. You will need these numbers.**

| | | | |
|---|---|---|---|
| cero = 0 | uno = 1 | dos = 2 | tres = 3 |
| cuatro = 4 | cinco = 5 | seis = 6 | diez = 10 |

# Pronunciation

## Words and sentences

**1** 🎧 **Listen to these words ending in a vowel, 's' or 'n'. Circle the syllable that has the stress.**

| | | |
|---|---|---|
| casa | casas | casan |
| habla | hablas | hablan |

**2** 🎧 **Listen to these words ending in a consonant (not 's' or 'n'). Circle the syllable that has the stress.**

| | | |
|---|---|---|
| hotel | hablar | profesor |
| Madrid | diez | |

**3** 🎧 **Listen to these words which have an accent. Circle the syllable that has the stress.**

| | |
|---|---|
| jardín | matemáticas |
| Almería | Los Ángeles |

**4** 🎧 **Listen and repeat. Notice how one word can run into the next.**

¿Dónde está?
Está en España.
Se llama Alberto.

**5** 🎧 **Be careful with words that look similar to English words. Say these words. Then listen and check.**

hotel   restaurante   tomate   David Beckham

**6** **Read these sentences aloud.**

Prefiero la comida italiana porque es deliciosa.
Mi plato favorito es la lasaña.
En un restaurante, como pasta y un helado de chocolate.

# 0.1 Quiz

**1** **Practise writing out these sentences, paying attention to the Spanish characters.**

 **a** ¿Cómo te llamas? _____

 **b** ¡Hola! Me llamo José María. _____

 **c** ¿Y tú? _____

 **d** Me llamo Iñigo. _____

**2** **Draw lines to match up.**

buenos     tardes

buenas     días

           noches

**3** 🎧 **Listen and identify the celebrities.**

_____  _____  _____  _____

**4** **Practise greeting and interviewing celebrities.**

¿Qué tal?

Me llamo …

¿Cómo te llamas?

Muy bien.

Buenas tardes.

¿Y tú?

Adiós.

**1** 🎧 Javier is planning a surprise party for his little brother. To keep it secret he spells out the important words. Listen and tick the ones he mentions.

fiesta ☐　　amigos ☐　　helado ☐　　hamburguesa ☐

iPod ☐　　música ☐　　osito ☐

**2** 🎧 Now spell out these other surprises. Listen and check.

> hamburguesa　iPod　móvil　juegos　osito

**3** Read and crack the code.

| tres | cuatro | cinco | seis | siete | ocho | nueve |
|------|--------|-------|------|-------|------|-------|
|      |        |       |      | *a*   |      |       |

a　h76bu5gu8s7 _____

b　58v9s37 _____

c　58g7l4 _____

d　64d7 _____

e　67sc437 _____

f　n757nj7 _____

g　s89s _____

h　s98t8 _____

**4** Colour all the masculine nouns in red and all the feminine ones in blue.

> unos amigos
>
> un regalo　　unas hamburguesas
>
> la fiesta　　un helado　　unas naranjas
>
> el deporte　　un grupo　　la música
>
> un pastel

**1** **Complete the grid. What do the words in the Plural column mean?**

*Ejemplo: mis padres = my parents.*

| Masculine | Feminine | Plural |
| --- | --- | --- |
| | | mis padres |
| mi tío | | |
| | | mis hermanos |
| mi abuelo | | |
| | mi prima | |

**2** **Read, then draw and label the family.**

> Me llamo Ana María. Tengo un hermanastro que se llama Javier. Mis padres se llaman Violeta y Juan Carlos. Mi madre tiene una hermana que se llama Teresa. Mi tía Teresa tiene un hijo que es mi primo Beto. Mi abuela, la madre de mi padre, se llama Ernestina.

**3** **Read and work out the meaning of the words in bold.**

Soy Ana María. Soy hija de Violeta y Juan Carlos. Soy la hermana de Javier. Soy la **nieta** de Ernestina. Soy la **sobrina** de Teresa y la prima de Beto.

_____          _____

**4** **Point to someone in your picture for Activity 2. Say five things about them.**

me llamo ...          Soy ...          Tengo ...          se llama ...

# 0.4  ¿Cuántos años tienes?

**1**  **Put these animals in order according to their lifespan. Use a dictionary to see what the animals are.**

Oso: cuarenta y tres años
Murciélago: veinticuatro años
Pato: veintinueve años
Gato: veinticinco años
Venado: veintiséis años
Loro: treinta años
Vaca: veintidós años
Zorro: catorce años
Lobo: dieciocho años
Burro: cuarenta y cinco años

|    |      |     |
|----|------|-----|
|    |      |     |
|    |      |     |
|    |      |     |
|    |      |     |
| 25 | Gato | Cat |
|    |      |     |
|    |      |     |
|    |      |     |
|    |      |     |

**2**  **Write your own answers to these questions.**

¿Qué tal? _____

¿Cómo te llamas? _____

¿Cuántos años tienes? _____

¿Tienes hermanos? _____

¿Tienes abuelos? _____

**3**  🎧 **Listen and answer the questions. Try not to get caught out. If you can, play the same game with a friend.**

**1**  Follow the word snake round the grid to read the conversation.
The snake can go up, down or across, but not diagonally.

| Q | u | é | n | g | e | s | h | o |
|---|---|---|---|---|---|---|---|---|
| l | a | t | e | o | n | e | e | c |
| c | e | l | t | t | r | i | r | i |
| ó | m | l | s | e | e | t | m | n |
| m | s | a | m | n | c | s | a | ú |
| o | a | m | o | e | e | o | n | o |
| t | l | a | p | i | a | ñ | o | j |
| e | l | d | e | t | s | n | s | i |
| c | o | r | o | s | o | o | y | h |
| u | á | n | t | a | ñ | s | o | |

**2**  Use this grid to make a Spanish conversation snake for a friend.

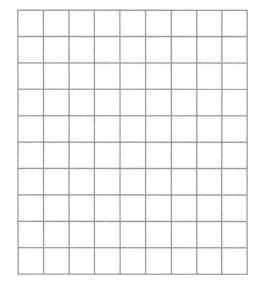

**Recuerdo**

In Spanish, all nouns are either masculine or feminine:
*un hermano*
*una hermana*

**1** **Circle all the nouns.**

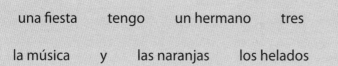

| | | | |
|---|---|---|---|
| una fiesta | tengo | un hermano | tres |
| la música | y | las naranjas | los helados |

I can only feel nouns in here!

**2** **How did you decide what was a noun? Give three ideas.**

_____

_____

_____

**3** **Sort these nouns into masculine and feminine by writing *un* or *una* in front of them. Use a dictionary to find out what they mean.**

_____ casa _____     _____ pulpo _____

_____ colegio _____     _____ piso _____

_____ camisa _____     _____ rana _____

_____ piscina _____     _____ bocadillo _____

_____ chico _____

**4** **A, the or some? Use the nouns in Activity 3 to translate these phrases into Spanish.**

the shirt _____     some boys _____

some frogs _____     the flat _____

a swimming pool _____     the houses _____

the sandwich _____     the octopus _____

**1** **Look at these two different vocabulary pages.**
**Decide who (Alex or Jordan) has …**

… recorded *un/una* with nouns        *Alex / Jordan*

… organised their words        *Alex / Jordan*

… given verbs in the infinitive form        *Alex / Jordan*

… kept Spanish and English clear        *Alex / Jordan*

… shown how words can change their endings        *Alex / Jordan*

… highlighted tricky areas        *Alex / Jordan*

… shown how words fit together in phrases        *Alex / Jordan*

> grandad un abuelo
> tengo I have
> dos hermano(s) two brothers
> a mother una madre
> a gran una abuela
> a(ñ)os years
> Alex

> abuelo/a – grandfather / mother
> hermano/a – brother / sister
> madre – mother
> tener – to have
>     tengo – I have
>     tengo un hermano
>     tengo doce años – I am twelve
> Jordan

**2** **What three things do you like about the way Alex has set out the vocabulary? And three things for Jordan?**

_____

_____

_____

_____

_____

_____

**3** **Record Alex and Jordan's vocabulary in the best possible way.**

| | |
|---|---|
| **¡Hola!** | **Hello!** |
| Saludos | Greetings |
| ¡Hola! | Hello! |
| Adiós | Goodbye |
| Hasta luego | See you later |
| Hasta pronto | See you soon |
| Soy Ana | I am Ana |
| Me llamo Federico | My name is Federico |

| | |
|---|---|
| **Durante la clase** | **In class** |
| escucha | listen |
| repite | repeat |
| habla | speak |
| lee | read |
| escribe | write |
| pregunta | ask |
| indica | point to |
| contesta | answer |
| mira | look |
| empareja | match |

| | |
|---|---|
| **Quiz** | **Quiz** |
| ¿Cómo te llamas? | What's your name? |
| Se llama Olivia | Her name is Olivia |
| ¿Qué tal? | How are you? |
| Buenos días | Good morning |
| Buenas tardes | Good afternoon |
| Buenas noches | Good night |

| | |
|---|---|
| **Me flipa; me molan** | **I love it; I'm into them** |
| uno | one |
| dos | two |
| tres | three |
| cuatro | four |
| cinco | five |
| seis | six |
| siete | seven |
| ocho | eight |
| nueve | nine |
| diez | ten |
| once | eleven |
| doce | twelve |
| trece | thirteen |
| catorce | fourteen |
| quince | fifteen |
| dieciséis | sixteen |
| diecisiete | seventeen |
| dieciocho | eighteen |
| diecinueve | nineteen |
| veinte | twenty |

| | |
|---|---|
| **La familia** | **The family** |
| el abuelo | grandfather |
| la abuela | grandmother |
| los abuelos | grandparents |

| | |
|---|---|
| mi padre | my father |
| mi madre | my mother |
| mis padres | my parents |
| el hermano | brother |
| la hermana | sister |
| el tío | uncle |
| la tía | aunt |
| el primo | cousin (m) |
| la prima | cousin (f) |
| el hermanastro | stepbrother |
| la hermanastra | stepsister |
| el padrastro | stepfather |
| la madrastra | stepmother |
| Soy hijo único | I'm an only child (m) |
| Soy hija única | I'm an only child (f) |

| | |
|---|---|
| **¿Cuántos años tienes?** | **How old are you?** |
| Tengo X años | I'm X years old |
| treinta | thirty |
| cuarenta | forty |
| cincuenta | fifty |
| sesenta | sixty |
| setenta | seventy |
| ochenta | eighty |
| noventa | ninety |
| cien | a hundred |

| | |
|---|---|
| **Gente y números** | **People and numbers** |
| hay | there is, there are |
| no hay | there isn't, there aren't |

## Checklist

| How well do you think you can do the following? | | | |
|---|---|---|---|
| Write a sentence for each one if you can. | | | |
| | I can do this well | I can do this but not very well | I can't do this yet |
| 1. Spell out loud | | | |
| 2. Count to 20 | | | |
| 3. Say the 10s up to 100 | | | |
| 4. Use *un/una/el/la* | | | |
| 5. Talk about family members | | | |
| 6. Say how old I am | | | |
| 7. Record vocabulary | | | |

**1** 🎧 Listen and play finger twister. When you hear a month, put a finger on it. Keep your fingers on the page. You will need all 10 fingers.

( enero )   ( febrero )   ( marzo )   ( abril )

( mayo )   ( junio )   ( julio )   ( agosto )

( septiembre )   ( octubre )   ( noviembre )   ( diciembre )

Shakira
2/2

Fernando Torres
20/3

Cesc Fàbregas
4/5

Madonna
16/8

Rio Ferdinand
7/11

Cristina Aguilera
18/12

**2** 🎧 Eva and José María are having a competition to see who knows the celebrities' birthdays. Listen and keep score.

| Eva | |
|---|---|
| José María | |

**3** Write a sentence in Spanish saying when each celebrity's birthday is.

*Ejemplo: El cumpleaños de Shakira es el dos de febrero.*

_____

_____

_____

_____

**1** 🎧 Listen to the English and Spanish ways of describing things, and try to tick which animal is being talked about.

 ☐  ☐  ☐  ☐  ☐  ☐

**2** Explain the difference between Spanish and English word order. Which order was more helpful in Activity 1 and why?

_____

_____

_____

**3** Read and underline all the pets, colours and numbers. These people are neighbours. How many pets do you think there are altogether?

> Tengo una tortuga, dos perros, y un gato que se llama Binki.

> Tenemos un gato blanco con ojos verdes, dos perros negros y un pez.

☐

> Tengo dos animales, un gato y un conejo. Los dos son blancos.

> Tengo un pájaro, un ratón, un pez ... y un gato blanco que se llama Monstruo.

> Tenemos un gato blanco que se llama Chispa, y un perro marrón.

**4** Draw lines to match up the colours to the animals and then draw them.

**a** Tengo un gato             negro

**b** Tengo dos perros          verde

**c** Tengo una tortuga         blancos

**d** Tengo tres arañas         rojas

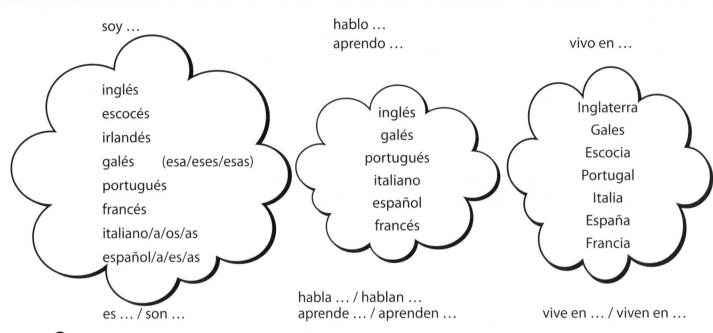

soy …

inglés
escocés
irlandés
galés     (esa/eses/esas)
portugués
francés
italiano/a/os/as
español/a/es/as

es … / son …

hablo …
aprendo …

inglés
galés
portugués
italiano
español
francés

habla … / hablan …
aprende … / aprenden …

vivo en …

Inglaterra
Gales
Escocia
Portugal
Italia
España
Francia

vive en … / viven en …

**1** 🎧 Listen and tick the words in the clouds as you hear them.

**2** 🎧 Listen again and fill in the information.

Nombre: *Tiago*
Nacionalidad:
Residencia:
Idiomas:
Madre:
Padre:

Nombre: *Violeta*
Nacionalidad:
Residencia:
Idiomas:
Madre:
Padre:

**3** Be Tiago or Violeta. Talk about yourself and your family in Spanish using the information you heard.

**4** Write up the information for the other person in full sentences.

_____

_____

_____

_____

_____

_____

**1** 🎧 **Listen to the descriptions of agents X, Y, Z and 0. Write the correct letter under each picture.**

**2** **Read the descriptions. Then draw the disguise on each agent.**

Agente X
Tiene una barba blanca y larga.

Agente Y
Tiene un bigote negro.

Agente Z
Lleva gafas.

Agente 0
Tiene una barba negra, un bigote y pecas.
Lleva una peluca larga y rubia, y gafas.

**una peluca –** *a wig*

**3** 🎧 **Listen. Which agent has been caught?**

**4** **Draw a picture of yourself before and after a disguise. Write a description in Spanish.**

**1**  Draw lines to match up the name of the country with the nationality.

| | |
|---|---|
| Méjico | argentino |
| Argentina | mejicano |
| Colombia | colombiano |
| Perú | venezolano |
| Venezuela | peruano |
| Guatemala | guatemalteco |
| Honduras | chileno |
| Chile | hondureño |

**2**  🎧 Listen and fill in the grid.

| Name | Nationality | Lives in | Language(s) |
|---|---|---|---|
| | | | |
| | | | |
| | | | |
| | | | |

**3**  🎧 In Latin America, a 'z' or a soft 'c' are pronounced like an 's'. In Spain, they are pronounced like an English 'th'. Try saying these sentences both ways, then listen to how Azucena and Cecilia say them.

**1**  Me llamo Azucena y soy venezolana. Vivo en Venezuela.

**2**  Me llamo Cecilia y vivo en Cádiz, una ciudad española.

## Recuerdo

In Spanish, verbs change their ending depending on the person doing the action of the verb.

**1** Find the infinitives and put them into three groups.

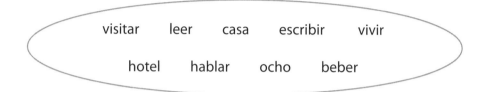

visitar   leer   casa   escribir   vivir

hotel   hablar   ocho   beber

| ar | er | ir |
|----|----|----|
|    |    |    |

**2** Listen and follow the instructions.

**3** Look at the *er* column below. Highlight what is different from the *ar* endings. Now look at the *ir* column. Highlight what is different from the *er* endings.

| ar | er | ir |
|----|----|----|
| o | o | o |
| as | es | es |
| a | e | e |
| amos | emos | imos |
| áis | éis | ís |
| an | en | en |

**4** Write out the verbs with the correct ending to complete the sentences.

**a** I visit my parents.    (Visitar) _____ a mis padres.

**b** We speak Spanish.    (Hablar) _____ español.

**c** He drinks water.    (Beber) _____ agua.

**d** They learn French.    (Aprender) _____ francés.

**Recuerdo**

Remember, only names (people, places, etc.) need a capital letter – unless it is the start of a sentence.

**1** Be the teacher. Elena has had some problems with getting capital letters right. Get out your red pen and correct her work.

> Me llamo Elena. Vivo en españa y soy Española. Hablo español y Francés. En el instituto tengo francés los Jueves y martes.

**2** Read Ryan's Spanish work. He has written a long list of pets. Can you rewrite it with connectives to make it a better piece of work?

> Tengo un gato y se llama Fernando y un perro y un pájaro y no tengo conejos, y mi hermano tiene un conejo y se llama Steven (el conejo, no mi hermano).
>
> _____
>
> _____
>
> _____
>
> _____

**3** Look at the pictures. Write a sentence for each one, using a quantifier.

a   b   c

> bastante – *quite*   un poco – *a bit*   muy – *very*   demasiado – *too*

_____

_____

_____

## Cumpleaños y fiestas — *Birthdays and festivals*

| | |
|---|---|
| enero | *January* |
| febrero | *February* |
| marzo | *March* |
| abril | *April* |
| mayo | *May* |
| junio | *June* |
| julio | *July* |
| agosto | *August* |
| septiembre | *September* |
| octubre | *October* |
| noviembre | *November* |
| diciembre | *December* |
| lunes | *Monday* |
| martes | *Tuesday* |
| miércoles | *Wednesday* |
| jueves | *Thursday* |
| viernes | *Friday* |
| sábado | *Saturday* |
| domingo | *Sunday* |

## Mis mascotas — *My pets*

| | |
|---|---|
| un ratón | *a mouse* |
| un pájaro | *a bird* |
| un gato | *a cat* |
| una rata | *a rat* |
| una tortuga | *a turtle / tortoise* |
| un perro | *a dog* |
| una araña | *a spider* |
| un pez | *a fish* |
| un conejo | *a rabbit* |
| un caballo | *a horse* |
| una cobaya | *a guinea pig* |
| una serpiente | *a snake* |
| blanco/a | *white* |
| negro/a | *black* |
| rojo/a | *red* |
| azul / verde | *blue / green* |
| amarillo/a | *yellow* |
| naranja / gris | *orange / grey* |
| marrón / rosa | *brown / pink* |
| morado/a | *purple* |

## Lenguas y nacionalidades — *Languages and nationalities*

| | |
|---|---|
| inglés / inglesa | *English* |
| escocés / escocesa | *Scottish* |
| irlandés / irlandesa | *Irish* |
| galés / galesa | *Welsh* |
| francés / francesa | *French* |
| español(a) | *Spanish* |
| portugués / portuguesa | *Portuguese* |
| italiano/a | *Italian* |

## ¿Cómo eres? — *What are you like?*

| | |
|---|---|
| Tengo … | *I have …* |
| el pelo | *hair* |
| largo / corto | *long / short* |
| liso / rizado | *straight / curly* |
| ondulado | *wavy* |
| de punta | *spiky* |
| los ojos | *eyes* |
| bigote / barba | *moustache / beard* |
| pecas | *freckles* |
| Llevo gafas | *I wear glasses* |
| Soy … | *I am …* |
| alto/a | *tall* |
| bajo/a | *short* |
| delgado/a | *slim* |
| gordo/a | *fat* |
| de talla mediana | *medium size* |
| (des)ordenado/a | *(un)tidy* |
| simpático/a | *friendly* |
| antipático/a | *unfriendly* |
| (im)paciente | *(im)patient* |
| estudioso/a | *studious* |
| perezoso/a | *lazy* |
| testarudo/a | *stubborn* |
| extrovertido/a | *outgoing* |
| tímido/a | *shy* |
| inteligente | *intelligent* |
| bobo/a | *silly* |
| (in)maduro/a | *(im)mature* |

## Checklist

| How well do you think you can do the following? | | | |
|---|---|---|---|
| Write a sentence for each one if you can. | | | |
| | I can do this well | I can do this but not very well | I can't do this yet |
| 1. Say dates and birthdays | | | |
| 2. Talk about pets and what colour they are | | | |
| 3. Make adjectives agree | | | |
| 4. Give your nationality and what languages you speak | | | |
| 5. Change verb endings | | | |
| 6. Describe yourself | | | |
| 7. Improve work with connectives and quantifiers | | | |

**1** 🎧 **Read aloud these words and then compare your pronunciation with the CD.**

**a** Words with accents:

> el ingl**é**s   la geograf**í**a   las matem**á**ticas   la inform**á**tica   la tecnolog**í**a

**b** Words with Spanish sounds:

> las **ci**en**ci**as   el espa**ñ**ol   la tecnolo**gí**a   la **ge**ografía   la **h**istoria

**2** **Masculine, feminine, singular, plural. Put the words below into the chart.**

| | Asignaturas | | Adjetivos |
|---|---|---|---|
| EL | | ES | *divertido* |
| LA | | | *divertida* |
| LOS | | SON | *divertidos* |
| LAS | | | *divertidas* |

> inglés       ciencias       dibujo
> español      deporte        geografía
> historia     matemáticas    informática
> tecnología   música

> útil           fácil        interesante
> aburrido       fáciles      difícil
> aburridas      útiles       difíciles
> interesantes   aburrida

**3** **Use the chart in Activity 2 to help you complete these sentences.**

**a** Me gusta el _____ porque es _____ .

**b** Me gusta la _____ porque es _____ .

**c** Me gustan las _____ porque son _____ .

**d** Me gusta _____ .

**e** Me gustan _____ .

**4** **Now read out your sentences from Activity 3, using these expressions to sound more personal.**

> para mí – *for me*      tan – *so*          muy – *very*
> un poco – *a bit*       demasiado – *too*   bastante – *quite*

**1** **Complete with the correct times.**

Son las _____.

Son las seis.

Son las dos.

Son las ocho.

Son las _____ y cuarto.

Son las dos y cuarto.

Son las seis y cuarto.

Son las siete y cuarto.

Son las _____ y media.

Son las tres y media.

Son las cuatro y media.

Son las diez y media.

Son las _____ menos cuarto.

Son las tres menos cuarto.

Son las ocho menos cuarto.

Son las seis menos cuarto.

**2** **Read and work out how many lessons Paula has each day. How long are the lessons? What time does she go home for lunch?**

> A las ocho tengo inglés. A las nueve menos cuarto tenemos deporte. Luego tengo matemáticas. A las diez y cuarto tenemos 15 minutos de recreo. A las diez y media tenemos español. Después tenemos una clase de geografía y una clase de historia. A la una menos cuarto tenemos ciencias, y a la una y media francés.

_____

_____

_____

**1**  🎧 **Guess the answers, then listen and see if you were right!**

**a**  Mi instituto es moderno / antiguo.

**b**  El patio es grande / pequeño.

**c**  Tenemos un aula especial para informática / tecnología.

**d**  Hay tres / cuatro oficinas.

**e**  La oficina del director / de la directora es grande.

**f**  Me gusta / No me gusta el instituto.

**g**  Hay / No hay un gimnasio.

**h**  Estudio en la biblioteca / el laboratorio.

**i**  Como en el patio / el comedor.

**2**  **Read this description then draw and label a plan of the school.**

> Mi instituto no es muy grande. Tenemos cinco aulas en total.
> La biblioteca es muy pequeña, pero tenemos un aula de informática
> con ordenadores. No hay gimnasio, pero hay un patio grande.
> Hay dos oficinas, una para el director y otra para la recepcionista.

**3**  **Adapt the ideas on this page to write a description of what there is in your own school.**

_____

_____

_____

_____

_____

# 1B.4 La ropa

**1** Carry out an experiment to evaluate different ways of learning clothes vocabulary.

**a** Learn these words by writing out the words eight times each. Try not to look at the word while you write. Check your spelling afterwards.

> un jersey – *jumper*    una corbata – *tie*    una falda – *skirt*

**b** Learn these words by recording them in Spanish and English on your phone, mp3 player or computer.

> un vestido – *dress*    una camisa – *shirt*    un chándal – *tracksuit*

**c** Learn these words by making a set of cards with words and pictures and testing yourself.

> unos zapatos – *shoes*    unos pantalones – *trousers*    una gorra – *hat*

**d** Learn these words by teaching them to a friend.

> unos calcetines – *socks*    una sudadera – *sweatshirt*    una chaqueta – *jacket*

**e** Learn these words by putting Spanish labels where you keep your clothes.

> unos vaqueros – *jeans*    una camiseta – *T-shirt*    un cinturón – *belt*

**2** When you have had time to learn all the words, do the test on the CD. Listen to the words and write them in English. Record your score for each set of words.

**a**  Score: ☐

**b**  Score: ☐

**c**  Score: ☐

**d**  Score: ☐

**e**  Score: ☐

**3** Use the technique that worked best for you to learn all the words on this page. Test yourself again with the CD.

Score: ☐

**1** Put these expressions into the correct column of the table.

> (es ... / son ...) difícil(es) aburrido/a/os/as interesante(s) fácil(es)
> me fascina(n) me interesa(n) me encanta(n) me gusta(n)
> saco buenas notas voy mal en ... soy fuerte en ... saco malas notas
> el profesor es simpático la profesora es simpática

| Positive | Negative |
|---|---|
|  |  |

**2** Explain why some of the words in the table have different options.

_____

_____

**3** 🎧 Listen to Pilar. Complete the grid with ☺ or ☹.

| la historia |  |
|---|---|
| las matemáticas |  |
| el inglés |  |
| las ciencias |  |
| la educación física |  |

**4** Give your own opinions of these subjects.

el español _____

la música _____

las ciencias _____

The endings of words help glue a sentence together in Spanish:
*Es un profesor simpático.*
*Es una profesora simpática.*

**1** Complete each sentence with an adjective. Make sure the ending agrees.

a La historia es _____ .

b Las matemáticas son _____ .

c El inglés es _____ .

d Los profesores son _____ .

The ending of a verb tells you which person is doing the action.

**2** Translate into English.

a Comemos en el comedor. _____

b El director come en su oficina. _____

c No llevo uniforme. _____

d Hablo con mis amigos. _____

e ¿Estudias español? _____

f Mis abuelos viven en España. _____

**3** Now change the sentences in Activity 2 to say the following.

a They eat … _____

b The teachers eat … _____

c We don't wear … _____

d She talks … _____

e Do you (plural) study … _____

f My grandmother lives … _____

**1** Copy out these words. Write three important things to remember about how to spell or pronounce each one.

| tecnología | geografía | matemáticas |
|---|---|---|
| historia | música | ciencias |

*Ejemplo: tecnología.* **1** *There is no 'h'*
**2** *There is an accent on the ía.*
**3** *Soft 'g' sound.*

_____

_____

_____

_____

_____

**2** A cognate is a word you can re<u>cogn</u>ise from a language you already know. How many of these words are cognates? Tick the ones that are.

| aula ☐ | gimnasio ☐ | laboratorio ☐ | patio ☐ |
|---|---|---|---|
| oficina ☐ | director ☐ | biblioteca ☐ | jersey ☐ |
| pantalón ☐ | chaqueta ☐ | corbata ☐ | camisa ☐ |

**3** Cognates help when you see the written word, but can be tricky when you need to use them yourself. Think about the words you ticked in Activity 2 and put them into the table in the correct column.

| Watch the spelling | Watch the pronunciation | Mean something slightly different |
|---|---|---|
| | | |
| | | |
| | | |
| | | |

## Mis asignaturas — *My subjects*

| | |
|---|---|
| la educación física | PE |
| el español | Spanish |
| el inglés | English |
| la geografía | geography |
| la historia | history |
| la informática | ICT |
| la tecnología | design and technology |
| las ciencias | science |
| las matemáticas | mathematics |
| fácil | easy |
| difícil | difficult |
| útil | useful |
| aburrido/a | boring |
| divertido/a | fun, amusing |
| interesante | interesting |
| un poco | a little |
| bastante | fairly, quite |
| tan | so |
| muy | very |
| demasiado | too (much) |
| para mí | for me |
| pero | but |
| me gusta | I like |
| te gusta | you like |
| correcto | true |
| mentira | false |

## La hora y el horario — *Time and timetable*

| | |
|---|---|
| Es la una | It is one o'clock. |
| ... y cinco | ... five past one |
| ... y cuarto | ... a quarter past one |
| ... y veinte | ... twenty past one |
| ... y media | ... half past one |
| Son las dos | It is two o'clock. |
| ... menos veinticinco | ... twenty-five to two |
| ... menos cuarto | ... a quarter to two |
| ... menos diez | ... ten to two |
| Es el mediodía | It is midday. |
| Es la medianoche | It is midnight. |

## Las instalaciones — *School buildings*

| | |
|---|---|
| el aula | the classroom |
| el gimnasio | the gym |
| el laboratorio | the laboratory |
| el patio | the playground |
| la biblioteca | the library |
| la oficina | the office |
| la oficina del director | the headteacher's office |
| grande | large |
| pequeño/a | small |
| moderno/a | modern |
| antiguo/a | old |
| bonito/a | attractive |
| feo/a | ugly |
| cómodo/a | comfortable |
| hay | there is / there are |

| | |
|---|---|
| leer un libro | to read a book |
| comer un bocadillo | to eat a sandwich |
| estudiar ciencias | to study science |
| charlar con amigos | to chat with friends |
| practicar deporte | to play sport |
| escribir cartas | to write letters |

## La ropa — *Clothes*

| | |
|---|---|
| llevar | to wear |
| un jersey | a jersey |
| una camisa | a shirt |
| una camiseta | a blouse |
| una corbata | a tie |
| una falda | a skirt |
| una sudadera | a sweatshirt |
| unas zapatillas | trainers |
| unos calcetines | socks |
| unos pantalones | trousers |
| unos vaqueros | jeans |
| unos zapatos | shoes |
| incómodo/a | uncomfortable |
| elegante | stylish |
| práctico/a | practical |
| formal | formal |
| feo/a | ugly |
| ridículo/a | ridiculous |
| informal | informal |

## Checklist

| How well do you think you can do the following? | | | |
|---|---|---|---|
| Write a sentence for each one if you can. | | | |
| | I can do this well | I can do this but not very well | I can't do this yet |
| 1. Give opinions about school subjects | | | |
| 2. Say what time lessons are | | | |
| 3. Say what is in your school | | | |
| 4. Describe your uniform | | | |
| 5. Change verb endings | | | |
| 6. Make adjectives agree | | | |
| 7. Use cognates to get a head start | | | |

**1** Put the weather words into the correct column.

| sol | llueve | frío | niebla | calor | nieva |
| buen tiempo | | tormenta | viento | mal tiempo | |

| hace ... | hay ... | |
| --- | --- | --- |

**2** 🎧 Listen and tick the correct weather for each day.

| lunes | martes | miércoles | jueves | viernes |
| --- | --- | --- | --- | --- |

**3** Roll a dice and see how quickly you can say the correct weather.

# 2A.2 Tiempo libre

**1** **Copy these activities, in order of personal preference.**

jugar al ajedrez _____

tocar la guitarra _____

jugar al tenis _____

ir al cine _____

practicar ciclismo _____

montar a caballo _____

bailar salsa _____

hacer windsurf _____

jugar con videojuegos _____

hacer atletismo _____

**2** **Go down your list of activities, giving an opinion about each one in Spanish. Use these words:**

| | |
|---|---|
| me gusta | y |
| me encanta | pero |
| me interesa | sin embargo |
| no me gusta | también |
| me aburre | además |
| me fastidia | |

*Ejemplo:* Me encanta ir al cine, pero ...

**3** **Finish these sentences, saying what you do and don't like to do.**

Si hace sol ... _____

Si hace calor ... _____

Si hace frío ... _____

Si llueve ... _____

Si hay tormenta ... _____

**1** **Write a Spanish caption under each picture.**

a

b

c

d

*Ejemplo: me despierto*

_____

_____

_____

e

f

g

h

_____

_____

_____

_____

**2** 🎧 **Listen to Javier playing a dice game. What has he 'forgotten' to do when he says he goes to school?**

⚀ Me lavo los dientes.          ⚃ Me visto.

⚁ Me ducho.                     ⚄ Me peino.

⚂ Desayuno.                     ⚅ Voy al instituto.

**3** **Now play the dice game yourself.**

**4** **Write up your random day from Activity 3. Use some of these words:**

> primero – *first*     luego – *next*     después – *afterwards*
> otra vez – *again*     finalmente – *finally*

_____

_____

_____

_____

**1**  **Read the list of activities. Are they things you do after school?**
**Put a tick or a cross.**

|  | Yo | Miriam |
|---|---|---|
| Veo la tele | ☐ | ☐ |
| Paseo al perro | ☐ | ☐ |
| Hago los deberes | ☐ | ☐ |
| Ceno | ☐ | ☐ |
| Meriendo | ☐ | ☐ |
| Descanso | ☐ | ☐ |
| Salgo | ☐ | ☐ |

**2**  🎧 **Listen to Miriam. Does she do the same things as you?**
**Tick the boxes for her.**

**3**  **Use your list to say what you do and don't do in the evening.**

*Ejemplo:*

Por la tarde …

Por la tarde no …

**4**  **Write about what you do in the evening. Use some of these words:**

a las …   luego   pero   entonces   finalmente

_____

_____

_____

_____

_____

# 2A.5 El fin de semana

**1** **What do you do at the weekend? Put these activities into the grid below.**

dormir hasta las diez

levantarme temprano

visitar a mi abuela

comer en un restaurante

hacer deporte

ver a mis amigos

salir con mi familia

| Puedo | No puedo |
|---|---|
| Me fastidia | Prefiero |

**2** 🎧 **Listen to Miriam. How would you describe her weekends? Explain why.**

_____

_____

**3** **Use the grid in Activity 1 to write a paragraph about your own weekends.**

> El fin de semana …   pero …   desafortunadamente …   porque …

_____

_____

_____

_____

_____

## Recuerdo

**Reflexive verbs.**
When you look at your reflection you see … yourself.
*Me lavo* – I wash myself
*Me visto* – I dress myself

**1** Explain why these words all have the same ending. Explain why they don't all start with *me*.

> me ducho  me visto  desayuno  me lavo

_____

_____

**2** Think like a Spanish person. Complete the grids.

*Ejemplo:*

| English | I get dressed |
| --- | --- |
| In betweenish | I dress myself |
| Spanish | Me visto |

| I get washed |
| --- |
|  |
| Me lavo |

| He has a shower |
| --- |
|  |
|  |

|  |
| --- |
| I wake myself up |
|  |

| I am called |
| --- |
|  |
|  |

**3** Translate into Spanish.

**a** He gets up. _____

**b** I wake up. _____

**c** Do you have a shower? _____

**d** They get dressed. _____

**Recuerdo**

All verbs change their endings. Some verbs also change part of their stem. These are called radical-changing verbs.

**Jugar (ue)**

| | |
|---|---|
| **jue**go | jugamos |
| **jue**gas | jugáis |
| **jue**ga | **jue**gan |

It is a good idea to note down the change like this: *Jugar (ue)*

**1** **Write out this verb in full:** *preferir (ie)*

_____     _____

_____     _____

_____     _____

**2** **Note the change in these verbs and write them out in the simplified way recommended in the *Recuerdo* box at the top of the page.**

querer – quiero, quieres, quiere, queremos, queréis, quieren _____

poder – puedo, puedes, puede, podemos, podéis, pueden _____

**3** **Give three reasons why it might be better to write *jugar (ue)* instead of writing out the whole verb.**

_____

_____

_____

**4** **Translate into Spanish.**

**a** I prefer _____

**b** We prefer _____

**c** You want _____

**d** He wants _____

**e** I can _____

**f** We can _____

## El tiempo — *The weather*

|  |  |
|---|---|
| hace buen tiempo | *it's fine / it's a nice day* |
| hace mal tiempo | *it's bad weather / it's not a nice day* |
| hace sol | *it's sunny* |
| hace calor | *it's hot* |
| hace frío | *it's cold* |
| hace viento | *it's windy* |
| hay tormenta | *it's stormy* |
| hay niebla | *it's foggy* |
| hay nubes | *it's cloudy* |
| llueve / nieva | *it's raining / it's snowing* |
| la primavera | *spring* |
| el verano | *summer* |
| el otoño | *autumn* |
| el invierno | *winter* |
| jugar a/al/a la | *to play* |
| el fútbol | *football* |
| el baloncesto | *basketball* |
| el ciclismo | *cycling* |
| el atletismo | *athletics* |
| el boxeo | *boxing* |
| la pelota vasca | *pelota* |
| el voleibol | *volleyball* |

## Tiempo libre — *Free time*

|  |  |
|---|---|
| ver la tele | *to watch TV* |
| salir con amigos | *to go out with friends* |
| tocar la guitarra | *to play the guitar* |
| ir al cine | *to go to the cinema* |
| montar a caballo | *to ride a horse* |
| bailar en la disco | *to dance in a disco* |
| jugar al ajedrez | *to play chess* |
| jugar con videojuegos | *to play computer games* |
| me apasiona | *I love* |
| me aburre | *it's boring* |
| me molesta | *it annoys me* |
| me fastidia | *it gets on my nerves* |
| navegar por internet | *to surf the net* |
| poder | *to be able* |
| preferir / prefiero | *to prefer / I prefer* |
| querer | *to like / want* |
| si | *if* |
| sí | *yes* |

## Por la mañana — *In the morning*

|  |  |
|---|---|
| levantarse | *to get up* |
| lavarse | *to get washed* |
| me lavo (los dientes) | *I clean (my teeth)* |
| ducharse | *to have a shower* |
| cepillarse | *to brush* |
| me cepillo (el pelo) | *I brush my hair* |
| peinarse | *to comb / do hair* |
| ponerse | *to put on (clothes)* |
| desayunar | *to have breakfast* |
| despertarse | *to wake up* |
| vestirse | *to dress* |
| almorzar (ue) | *to have lunch* |

## Por la tarde — *In the afternoon*

|  |  |
|---|---|
| a las trece horas | *at 13:00 hours (1 p.m.)* |
| descansar | *to relax* |
| merendar (ie) | *to have a snack* |
| pasear al perro | *to walk the dog* |
| hacer los deberes | *to do homework* |
| cenar | *to have supper* |
| acostarse (ue) | *to go to bed* |
| dormirse (ue) | *to fall asleep* |
| ir | *to go* |
| hacer compras | *to do the shopping* |
| la piscina | *swimming pool* |
| nadar | *to swim* |

## El fin de semana — *(At) the weekend*

|  |  |
|---|---|
| hasta las diez | *until ten o' clock* |
| tarde / temprano | *late / early* |
| de acuerdo | *agreed* |
| montar en bicicleta | *to ride a bike* |
| el sábado | *on Saturday* |
| los sábados | *on Saturdays* |
| la cocina | *kitchen* |
| las tostadas | *toast* |
| los cereales | *cereal* |
| en tren | *by train* |
| frente a | *opposite* |
| el mar | *the sea* |
| pasarlo bomba | *to have a great time* |

## Checklist

| How well do you think you can do the following? Write a sentence for each one if you can. | I can do this well | I can do this but not very well | I can't do this yet |
|---|---|---|---|
| 1. Talk about the weather | | | |
| 2. Say what you like and don't like doing | | | |
| 3. Say what you do in the morning, evening and at weekends | | | |
| 4. Use radical-changing verbs | | | |
| 5. Use reflexive verbs | | | |
| 6. Record information on verbs | | | |

**1** Write a caption for each picture.

a

la _____ ☐

b

la _____ ☐

c

la _____ ☐

d

el _____ ☐

**2** 🎧 Listen. Where do they live? Write the correct number in each box above.

**3** Randomsville: Toss a coin to see what is in the town.

> Heads = *Hay* ... (there is). Tails = *No hay* ... (there isn't).

*Ejemplo:*  「 Hay un supermercado ... 」

un supermercado          una piscina          un hospital

un museo                    un parque

un zoo          una bolera          un colegio

**4** Use these words to write sentences about Randomsville.

| Es ... | | Está ... | |
|---|---|---|---|
| una ciudad | histórico | en la costa | en el sur |
| un pueblo | tranquilo | en el campo | en el oeste |
| grande | moderno | en la montaña | en el este |
| pequeño | industrial | en España | en el centro |
| | | en el norte | |

_____

_____

_____

**1** **Do the maths.**

*Ejemplo: to + the = to the*

a + el = _____

a + los = _____

a + la = _____

a + las = _____

**2** **Put the words into the grid. Then use it to make up sentences.**

| Voy | al | | con mis amigos. |
| | | | con mi familia. |
| | a la | | los sábados. |
| | | | todos los días. |
| | a los | | a veces. |
| | | | de vez en cuando. |
| | a las | | a menudo. |

supermercado    tiendas    piscina    bolera    parque
grandes almacenes    oficina de Correos    instituto

**3** 🎧 **Listen and do the actions.**

**4** **Put on your favourite song. Make up 'a la izquierda' actions to go with it. Write down the instructions.**

_____

_____

_____

_____

**1** **Read and underline all the names of rooms.**

Hola, soy Carmen. Voy a describir mi casa. La entrada está en la planta baja.
Al entrar, a la izquierda está la cocina, y enfrente está el comedor. Al lado
del comedor, o sea la segunda habitación a la derecha, está el salón. Es un
salón muy grande. Enfrente del salón está el despacho de mi padre y hay un
cuarto de baño.
En la primera planta están los dormitorios. Mis padres tienen el dormitorio
grande. Enfrente del dormitorio de mis padres hay otro cuarto de baño y un
salón con un televisor grande. Al final, a la izquierda está el dormitorio de
mi hermano, y a la derecha tengo mi dormitorio.

**2** **Read again, and draw in the rooms on this plan.**

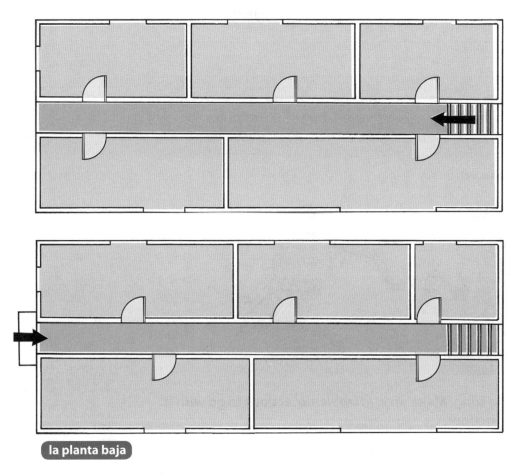

la planta baja

**3** 🎧 **Listen and add the five extra details to the plan.**

**1** 🎧 **Listen to the four friends. Number each picture correctly.**

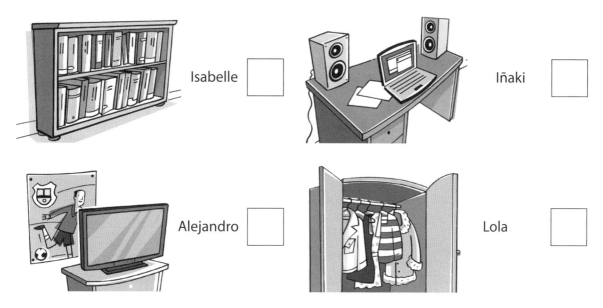

Isabelle ☐    Iñaki ☐

Alejandro ☐    Lola ☐

**2** **Use this grid to talk about your own bedroom.**

| En mi dormitorio tengo … En mi dormitorio hay … No tengo … | un armario un escritorio un televisor un ordenador una cama una lámpara una alfombra una silla | muy un poco no muy demasiado bastante | grande pequeño/a elegante moderno/a bonito/a |
|---|---|---|---|
| y      pero      también | al lado de      encima de      en | | |

**3** **Write a short description of your room.**

_____

_____

_____

_____

**1** Find four words to describe each picture.

a

b

c

_____

_____

_____

_____

> museos   industrial   granjas   turistas   pintoresco   tranquilo
> animado   gente   verde   monumentos   paisaje   tráfico

**2** Follow the word snake round the first grid to find a sentence. Then make up your own word snake sentence to describe a place.

| → E | s | c | h | y | m | u |
|---|---|---|---|---|---|---|
| u | m | u | o | s | o | s |
| y | n | m | s | m | t | e |
| p | o | c | o | o | n | o |
| i | o | r | c | n | e | s |
| n | t | e | s | u | m |   |

_____

_____

_____

> Es ...   muy ...   con ...
> hay ...   muchos ...   y ...

**1** **Write out the two verbs.**

| to be (permanent quality) | ser |
|---|---|
| I am | |
| | |
| | |
| | |
| | |

| to be (position or temporary state) | estar |
|---|---|
| I am | |
| | |
| | |
| | |
| | |

eres  está  es  estamos  somos  estáis  soy
estoy  estás  sois  son  están

**2** 🎧 **Listen and check. Then listen and repeat with actions.**

*Ser* – on each person, bang your hand on the table to show it is permanent.
*Estar* – on each person, wobble your hand to show it is a temporary state.

**3** **Decide which words go with *soy* … and which go with *estoy* … Then write out the words in sentences with *soy* and *estoy*.**

español(a) – *Spanish*
enfermo/a – *ill*
triste – *sad*
en mi casa – *at home*

bastante inteligente – *quite intelligent*
de Madrid – *from Madrid*
estudiante – *a student*
en la cama – *in bed*

_____

_____

_____

_____

**1**   **Find the information in this Spanish address.**

```
Ana García López
C/ Luís Roldán 23, 3° izq.
50012 ZARAGOZA
(Aragón)
```

Her first name is _____.

Her surnames are _____ (her father's surname)

and _____ (her mother's surname).

She lives at number _____ on _____ Street,

on the _____ floor, on the _____.

Her postcode is _____.

The city is _____.

The region is _____.

**2**   **Now write out the name and address of someone you know, using the Spanish style.**

_____

_____

_____

_____

| **Vivo en ...** | **I live in ...** |
|---|---|
| Está en ... | It is in ... |
| la montaña | the mountains |
| la costa | the coast |
| el campo | the countryside |
| la ciudad | the city |
| un pueblo | a town |
| una aldea | a village |
| un barrio | a neighbourhood |
| las afueras | the outskirts |

| **¿Dónde está?** | **Where is it?** |
|---|---|
| siempre | always |
| todos los días | every day |
| a menudo | often |
| a veces | sometimes |
| nunca | never |
| una vez a la semana | once a week |
| dos veces a la semana | twice a week |
| un supermercado | a supermarket |
| un parque | a park |
| una estación | a station |
| un banco | a bank |
| un museo | a museum |
| una catedral | a cathedral |
| un zoo | a zoo |
| un colegio | a school |
| un cine | a cinema |
| un parque de atracciones | a theme park |
| la bolera | the bowling alley |
| el polideportivo | the sports centre |
| la piscina | the swimming pool |
| la oficina de Correos | the post office |
| el ayuntamiento | the town hall |
| la iglesia | the church |
| los grandes almacenes | the department store |
| la parada de autobús | the bus stop |
| las tiendas | the shops |
| Sigue / Siga | Carry on |
| Todo recto | Straight ahead |
| Tuerce / Tuerza | Turn |
| Cruza / Cruce | Cross |
| Toma / Tome | Take |
| el puente | the bridge |
| la primera / segunda / tercera | the first / second / third |
| la calle | the street |
| a la derecha / izquierda | on the right / left |

| **Mi casa** | **My house** |
|---|---|
| un sótano | a basement |
| la planta baja | the ground floor |
| la primera planta | the first floor |
| el ático | the attic |
| una entrada | an entrance hall |
| las escaleras | the stairs |

| | |
|---|---|
| una cocina | a kitchen |
| un salón | a living room |
| un comedor | a dining room |
| un dormitorio | a bedroom |
| un cuarto de baño | a bathroom |
| una ducha | a shower |
| un aseo | a toilet |
| un despacho | an office |
| un jardín | a garden |
| un balcón | a balcony |
| una piscina | a swimming pool |

| **Mi dormitorio** | **My bedroom** |
|---|---|
| un armario | a wardrobe |
| una cama | a bed |
| un escritorio | a desk |
| unas estanterías | a bookcase / some shelves |
| una mesita de noche | a bedside table |
| una alfombra | a rug |
| una cómoda | a chest of drawers |
| una silla | a chair |
| unas cortinas | curtains |
| una puerta | a door |
| una ventana | a window |
| una lámpara | a lamp |
| delante de | in front of |
| enfrente de | facing |
| detrás de | behind |
| encima de | on / on top of |
| debajo de | under |
| entre | between |
| al lado de | next to |
| cerca de / lejos de | near to / far from |

## Checklist

| How well do you think you can do the following? | | | |
|---|---|---|---|
| Write a sentence for each one if you can. | | | |
| | I can do this well | I can do this but not very well | I can't do this yet |
| 1. Say where you live | | | |
| 2. Talk about what there is in your town | | | |
| 3. List the rooms in your house | | | |
| 4. Say where the rooms are | | | |
| 5. Talk about your bedroom | | | |
| 6. Use *ser* and *estar* | | | |
| 7. Read a Spanish address | | | |

**1**  **Write the Spanish for these foods.**

  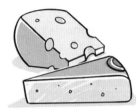  

_____  _____  _____

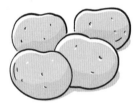    

_____  _____  _____

**2**  **Think like a Spanish person. Fill in the grids.**

*Ejemplo:*

| English | *garlic bread* | roast chicken |
|---|---|---|
| In betweenish | *bread of garlic* | |
| Spanish | *pan de ajo* | |

| | | |
|---|---|---|
| | potatoes fried | |
| un bocadillo de queso | | chile con carne |

**3**  **Write the Spanish for the following.**

a ham sandwich _____

roast meat _____

a chocolate cake _____

a fried egg _____

> jamón – *ham*      un pastel – *a cake*      un huevo – *an egg*
> asado/a/os/as – *roast*      frito/a/os/as – *fried*

**comida italiana**

**pescado**

**comida malsana**

**comida deliciosa**

**mariscos**

**comida sana**

**fruta**

**1** 🎧 **Listen. For each category of food mentioned, see how many different foods you can say. Use vocabulary page 55 to help (or page 103 of the Students' Book).**

*Ejemplo: Comida italiana: pizza, pasta, pan de ajo …*

**2** **Read. Then answer the questions in English.**

> Lionel
> Me gusta comer postres, pero no me gusta mucho la fruta. Prefiero helados o pasteles. Contienen mucho azúcar, pero me gustan.

> Cristiano
> Me gusta la comida rápida. Me encanta comer hamburguesas, patatas fritas. Está bien, porque no como postres ni bombones.

> Magda
> Me gusta comer fruta y verduras. No como carne y no como pescado.

**a** Who has the healthiest diet, and why?

_____

**b** Who knows they have an unhealthy diet? Why don't they change?

_____

**c** Who thinks their diet is OK? How do they justify it?

_____

**3** **Write about what healthy and unhealthy foods you like to eat.**

_____

_____

_____

_____

_____

**1**  🎧 **Listen to the two people ordering food. Who do you think they are? Tick the ones you think they might be.**

an athlete ☐

a British tourist ☐

a supermodel ☐

your teacher ☐

a millionaire ☐

**2**  **Create a special menu (in Spanish) for each of the three other people on the list in Activity 1.**

Comida

Bebida

Comida

Bebida

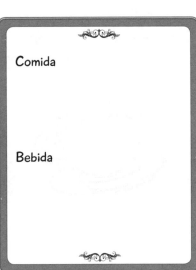

Comida

Bebida

**3**  **Order for the three people in Activity 2 from the menus.**

(no) tengo / tiene hambre ...   (no) tengo / tiene sed ...
¡oiga!                          para mí ...    para él ...    para ella ...
quiero ...                      quiere ...
para beber ...                  para comer ...
gracias

**1** **Read the jokes and find these words in Spanish.**

| | | | |
|---|---|---|---|
| a fly | _____ | soup | _____ |
| a spider | _____ | there is | _____ |
| I'm sorry | _____ | to eat | _____ |
| lifeguard | _____ | I don't have any | _____ |
| today | _____ | a mouse | _____ |

**1**

– ¡Oiga, camarero! Hay una mosca en mi sopa.
– Lo siento, señor. ¿Es usted vegetariano?

**2**

– ¡Oiga, camarero! Hay una araña en mi sopa.
– ¿Una araña? Sí, le gusta comer moscas.

**3**

– ¡Oiga, camarero! Hay un ratón en mi sopa.
– Lo siento. No tengo moscas hoy.

**4**

– ¡Oiga, camarero! Hay una mosca muerta en mi sopa.
– ¡Oiga, señor, soy camarero, no soy socorrista!

**2** **Translate each of the jokes into English.**

**1** _____

_____

**2** _____

_____

**3** _____

_____

**4** _____

_____

**3** 🎧 **Listen to the jokes and underline any words you think are tricky to pronounce. Listen again and repeat these tricky words.**

**4** **Practise telling the jokes until you can read them aloud perfectly and you know at least one off by heart. Record it on your phone or mp3, or tell it to your teacher.**

# 3A.5 Me encanta la comida

**1** **Read about the foods and identify what they are.**

**a** Se come mucho en Italia. Es deliciosa. Contiene pan, tomate, queso, jamón, aceitunas… Se come caliente y con ensalada.  _____

**b** Se come mucho en Inglaterra. Contiene carne o verduras. Es muy picante. Se come con arroz.  _____

**c** Se come mucho en Francia. Contiene harina, huevos y leche. Es dulce. Se come con limón y azúcar.  _____

**d** Se come en el Japón. Contiene pescado crudo y arroz. A veces contiene algas. Es muy sano.  _____

**2** **Explain some English dishes to a Spanish person.**

> Toad in the Hole    Ploughman's Lunch    Shepherd's Pie

> se come en …    se come con …    es …    contiene …

_____

_____

_____

_____

_____

_____

_____

_____

## Recuerdo

In Spanish, there is a formal word for 'you'. It uses the third person instead of the second:

*¿Tienes pulgas?* → *¿Tiene pulgas?*
Do you have fleas? → Do you have fleas? (formal)

In English the Queen is addressed in the third person:

'Does your Majesty have …?'

**1**   **Change the informal form into the formal form.**

| Informal – 2nd person | Formal – 3rd person |
| --- | --- |
| tienes | |
| deseas | |

**2**   **Join up the pairs that mean the same thing. Circle the ones that are in the formal form.**

Aquí tiene. – *Here you are.*

¿Y para ti? – *And for you?*

¿Tienes …? – *Do you have any …?*

¿Qué va a tomar? – *What are you going to have?*

¿Quiere …? – *Do you want …?*

¿Qué deseas? – *What would you like?*

¿Qué vas a tomar?

¿Quieres …?

¿Qué desea?

Aquí tienes.

¿Y para usted?

¿Tiene …?

**3**   🎧 **Listen. Formal or informal? Circle the correct one.**

**1**   Formal / Informal

**2**   Formal / Informal

**3**   Formal / Informal

**1**   **Look at the vocabulary on page 55 (or page 103 in the Students' Book). Make yourself a memory jogging recipe by putting together ingredients that begin with the same letter of the alphabet.**

*Ejemplo:*
*atún, arroz, azúcar*

un café con chocolate … y carne

| **Es la hora de comer** | **It's time to eat** |
|---|---|
| la cena | evening meal |
| la comida | midday meal |
| la merienda | (afternoon) snack |
| a eso de | at about |
| el chocolate | chocolate |
| el pan de ajo | garlic bread |
| la carne | meat |
| las verduras | vegetables |
| los cereales | cereal |
| los churros | churros |
| un bocadillo de queso | cheese sandwich |
| un paquete de patatas fritas | packet of crisps |
| un pollo asado | roast chicken |
| una paella | paella |
| una pizza | pizza |

| **Comida sana** | **Healthy food** |
|---|---|
| el atún | tuna |
| los mariscos | shellfish |
| el pescado | fish |
| el salmón | salmon |
| las gambas | prawns |
| los calamares | squid |
| un melocotón | peach |
| un plátano | banana |
| una ensalada verde | green salad |
| una manzana | apple |
| una naranja | orange |
| contiene mucha grasa | it contains a lot of fat |
| contiene mucho azúcar | it contains a lot of sugar |
| es (muy) … | it's (very) |
| … sano/a | healthy |
| … malsano/a | unhealthy |
| … soso/a | bland |
| … delicioso/a | delicious |
| son (muy) … | they are (very) |
| … sanos/as | healthy |
| … malsanos/as | unhealthy |
| … sosos/as | bland |
| … deliciosos/as | delicious |

| **¡Tengo hambre!** | **I'm hungry!** |
|---|---|
| una coca-cola | a coca-cola |
| una fanta naranja | fizzy orange |
| un café solo | black coffee |
| un café con leche | white coffee |
| un vaso de vino tinto | a glass of red wine |
| un vaso de vino blanco | a glass of white wine |
| una cerveza | a beer |

| un agua mineral con gas | sparkling mineral water |
|---|---|
| un agua mineral sin gas | still mineral water |
| tengo hambre | I'm hungry |
| tengo sed | I'm thirsty |
| para comer | to eat |
| para beber | to drink |

| **¡Oiga, camarero!** | **Waiter!** |
|---|---|
| una cuchara | a spoon |
| un tenedor | a fork |
| un cuchillo | a knife |
| ¿Dónde está …? | Where is …? |
| pedí | I asked for |
| hay | there is |
| una mosca | a fly |
| lo siento | I'm sorry |
| lo traigo | I'll bring it |
| en seguida | at once |
| traigo otro | I'll bring another |

| **Me encanta la comida** | **I love food** |
|---|---|
| el arroz | rice |
| la pasta | pasta |
| las especias | spices |
| es muy / es poco | it's very / it's not very |
| contiene mucho | it contains a lot (of) |
| contiene poco | it contains little (not a lot of) |
| utiliza mucho | it uses a lot (of) |
| utiliza poco | it uses little (not a lot of) |

# Checklist

| How well do you think you can do the following? | | | |
|---|---|---|---|
| Write a sentence for each one if you can. | | | |
| | I can do this well | I can do this but not very well | I can't do this yet |
| 1. Talk about mealtimes | | | |
| 2. Talk about healthy food | | | |
| 3. Say what you like to eat | | | |
| 4. Order food in a café | | | |
| 5. Complain in a café | | | |
| 6. Describe food from different countries | | | |
| 7. Create memory joggers | | | |

**1** **Write the correct words under each picture.**

a

*Ejemplo: en coche*

b

c

d

e

f

g

h
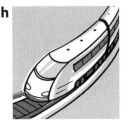

i

**2** 🎧 **Listen and select a suitable form of transport for each person.**

1 ☐   2 ☐   3 ☐

4 ☐   5 ☐   6 ☐

**3** **Write up your answers to Activity 2 in sentences, explaining why.**

*Ejemplo: Voy al instituto en tren porque es más rápido.*

_____

_____

_____

_____

_____

_____

rápido   conveniente   cómodo   fácil   barato   divertido   corto

# 3B.2 Alojamiento

**1** 🎧 **Listen. Find the right word and say it as soon as you can.**

a un camping
b un hotel
c un albergue juvenil
d una habitación
e sábanas
f una pensión

**2** **Read and decide what is being described (a–f) in each advert.**

1 Cinco estrellas, restaurante, piscina, canchas de tenis, 530 habitaciones. ☐

2 Cerca de la playa. Duchas, piscina, parking para coches, sitio para tiendas o caravanas. ☐

3 Balcón, cuarto de baño con ducha, una cama doble y vistas al mar. Televisor y un minibar. ☐

4 Barato y básico, perfecto para jóvenes que quieren explorar el campo. ☐

**3** **Write a sentence about each place in Activity 2.**

*Ejemplo: Voy a [una pensión] porque está cerca del mar, pero es muy barata.*

_____
_____
_____
_____

(no) voy a … hay … tiene … es … está …

**1**    **Read and note all the details in English.**

Estimado Señor,

Quiero hacer una reserva en su hotel, para una familia de cuatro personas: Dos adultos y dos niños de seis y ocho años. Es para tres noches, del ocho al once de agosto. En las habitaciones, queremos un baño para los niños y una habitación con ducha para los adultos. Queremos tener una televisión y WiFi en la habitación. Vamos a comer en el restaurante del hotel, y tengo que avisarle de que somos vegetarianos. Espero que no presente ningún problema.

Atentamente,

**2**    **Write a similar letter for this family.**

4-9 julio

Estimado Señor,

_____

_____

_____

_____

_____

Atentamente,

**1**  **Try to match up the sentence halves.**

1 Voy a ir a ☐     **a** una tienda.

2 Voy a trabajar en ☐     **b** la piscina.

3 Voy a alojarme en ☐     **c** un hotel.

4 Voy a nadar en ☐     **d** museos.

5 Voy a visitar ☐     **e** España.

**2**  🎧 **Listen and check.**

**3**  **Read the information. Traffic light the sentences:**

Underline in green = I understand it.
Underline in orange = I know what it is about.
Underline in red = I don't know what it is about.

> Dalí fue un pintor español muy famoso. El Museo Dalí está en Figueres, al norte de Barcelona. En junio, julio, agosto y septiembre el museo está abierto de 9h a 20h los siete días de la semana. De octubre a mayo está abierto de 10.30h a 18h, de martes a domingo. No está abierto el 25 de diciembre ni el 1 de enero. Los niños de 0 a 8 años entran gratis y hay descuentos para estudiantes y jubilados (de más de 60 años). Figueres está a 100 kilómetros de Barcelona. En tren o en coche, es un viaje de una hora y media. Si vas en tren, el museo está a 15 minutos andando de la estación de Figueres.

**4**  **Translate your green sentences. Give one piece of information for each orange sentence. Make an intelligent guess as to what each red sentence is about.**

_____

_____

_____

_____

_____

_____

_____

**1** **Read and fill in the missing question words.**

**a** ¿_____ vas de vacaciones? – Where are you going on holiday?

**b** ¿_____ vas a ir? – When are you leaving?

**c** ¿_____ tiempo vas a estar allí? – How long are you going to be there?

**d** ¿_____ vas a viajar? – How are you going to travel?

**e** ¿_____ tiempo hace en agosto? – What is the weather like in August?

**f** ¿_____ vas a hacer? – What are you going to do?

> Qué   Cómo   Adónde   Cuánto   Cuándo   Qué

**2** **Find these question words in Activity 1.**

**a** where         _____

**b** when          _____

**c** how           _____

**d** what          _____

**e** how long      _____

**3** 🎧 **Listen and note the answer to each question in Spanish.**

1 _____        4 _____

2 _____        5 _____

3 _____        6 _____

**4** 🎧 **Listen to the questions. Use your answers to Activity 3 to reply in Spanish in full sentences. Then listen again and give your own answers.**

## Recuerdo

Use 'going to' to talk about the future.
For example:

*Ejemplo:*

| _I_ | Voy | a | nadar en la piscina. |
| | Vas | a | salir con tus amigos. |
| | Va | a | ir de vacaciones. |
| | Vamos | a | comer a la una. |
| | Vais | a | viajar a Colombia. |
| | Van | a | jugar al baloncesto. |

**1** Write the correct person next to the verb in the examples above.

**2** Translate the examples in the *Recuerdo* box into English.

*Ejemplo: I am going to swim in the pool.*

_____

_____

_____

_____

_____

**3** Translate the following into Spanish.

**a** I am going to eat in a restaurant. _____

**b** She is going to visit a museum. _____

**c** We are going to travel by plane. _____

**d** They are going to work in a café. _____

**e** She is going to stay in a hotel. _____

**f** You are going to go shopping. _____

**1** 🎧 **Listen and tick off any words in the boxes that you hear.**

| | |
|---|---|
| me gusta | puedo |
| me encanta | voy a |
| quiero | prefiero |
| me gustaría | no … |

| | |
|---|---|
| ir | alojarme |
| visitar | viajar |
| ir de compras | salir |
| explorar | nadar |
| sacar fotos | comer |

| | |
|---|---|
| en un restaurante | a España |
| en un hotel | en la piscina |
| a la playa | con mis amigos |
| en la ciudad | con mi familia |

**2** **Your turn. Start with '*Voy a ir a España …*' then roll a dice for a connective. Carry on for as long as you can.**

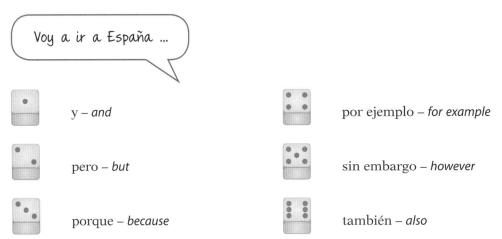

Voy a ir a España …

| | |
|---|---|
| ⚀ | y – *and* |
| ⚁ | pero – *but* |
| ⚂ | porque – *because* |
| ⚃ | por ejemplo – *for example* |
| ⚄ | sin embargo – *however* |
| ⚅ | también – *also* |

## El transporte — Transport

| El transporte | Transport |
| --- | --- |
| en autobús (el) | by bus |
| en metro (el) | by underground |
| en barco (el) | by boat |
| en bicicleta (la) | by bike |
| en tren (el) | by train |
| en avión (el) | by plane |
| en coche (el) | by car |
| en autocar (el) | by coach |
| un viaje | a journey |
| viajar | to travel |
| cómodo/a | comfortable |
| barato/a | cheap |
| corto/a | short |
| divertido/a | amusing |
| un billete | a ticket |
| ida y vuelta | return |
| cada veinte minutos | every 20 minutes |
| tardar | to take time |

## Alojamiento — Accommodation

| Alojamiento | Accommodation |
| --- | --- |
| alojarse | to board / to stay |
| un albergue juvenil | youth hostel |
| una pensión | bed and breakfast |
| un camping | campsite |
| quedarse | to stay |
| vale la pena | it's worth it |
| antiguo/a | ancient / old |
| tan … como | as … as |
| mejor | better |
| el/la mejor | the best |
| peor | worse |
| el/la peor | the worst |
| la sábana | sheet |
| la habitación | room |
| el ascensor | lift |

## Quiero reservar … — I want to reserve …

| Quiero reservar … | I want to reserve … |
| --- | --- |
| reservar | to reserve / to book |
| una reserva | a booking |
| confirmar | to confirm |
| incluido | included |
| el precio | the price |
| cerrar | to close |
| cerrado/a | closed |
| abrir | to open |
| abierto/a | open |
| una plaza | a camping plot |
| una tienda | a tent |
| incluso | inclusive |
| acampar | to pitch a tent |

## ¿Adónde vamos? — Where shall we go?

| ¿Adónde vamos? | Where shall we go? |
| --- | --- |
| precioso/a | pretty |
| maravilloso/a | marvellous |
| cada | each / every |
| media hora | half hour |
| apreciar | to appreciate |
| una parada | stop (bus) |
| perderse | to get lost |
| encontrarse | to meet / find each other |
| el dinero | money |
| tener suerte | to be lucky |
| menores de | under the age of |
| la estación | station |
| nace | is born |
| se casa con | marries |
| un juguete | toy |
| inolvidable | unforgettable |
| divertido/a | amusing |
| genial | great |
| fatal | awful |
| sensacional | amazing |
| guay | cool |
| pasarlo bomba | to have a great time |
| un parque de atracciones | fun fair / theme park |
| el mercado | market |
| antiguo/a | ancient |
| un guía | a guide (person) |
| una guía | a guide book |
| orientarse | to find your way |
| guardar | to keep (safe) |
| vigilar | to look after |
| una torre | tower |
| una tumba | tomb |
| las normas | rules and regulations |

## Checklist

| How well do you think you can do the following? | | | |
| --- | --- | --- | --- |
| Write a sentence for each one if you can. | | | |
| | I can do this well | I can do this but not very well | I can't do this yet |
| 1. Compare forms of transport | | | |
| 2. Use 'going to' to talk about the future | | | |
| 3. Book holiday accommodation | | | |
| 4. Talk about holiday activities | | | |
| 5. Extend your answers | | | |

**a**  ☐

**b**  ☐

**c**  ☐

**d**  ☐

**e** ☐

**f**  ☐

**g**  ☐

**1** 🎧 **Listen to what you can and can't do in the town. Tick or cross each picture.**

**2** **Use your answers to Activity 1 to talk in sentences about the town.**

> Se puede …

> No se puede …

> porque hay …

> porque no hay …

**3** **Write a paragraph about what you can and can't do in your own town and why.**

| | | | |
|---|---|---|---|
| porque … | puesto que … | pues … | ya que … |
| hay … | tiene … | tenemos … | es … |

_____
_____
_____
_____
_____
_____
_____

**1** 🎧 **Put the parts of the verb into the correct order. Then listen and check.**

> fuisteis    fue    fuiste    fui    fuimos    fueron

I went _____

you went _____

he/she/it went _____

we went _____

you (plural) went _____

they went _____

**2** **Translate into English.**

**a** Marisa fue a Argentina. Fue en agosto. Fue en avión. Fue a visitar a su familia.

_____

_____

**b** Fuimos a España. Fuimos en julio. Fuimos a la playa. Fuimos en coche.

_____

_____

**c** Mis amigos fueron a Francia. Fueron en barco. Fueron en abril. Fueron a París.

Fueron de compras. _____

_____

**3** **Now write five short sentences about your own holiday. Where? When? Where exactly? Who with? What did you go to do?**

_____

_____

_____

_____

_____

**1**  **Read and underline the six preterite endings.**

> El año pasado fui a España. Normalmente voy a Málaga, pero decidí ir a Madrid. Normalmente voy a la playa, pero en Madrid visité galerías de arte. Comí en unos restaurantes fantásticos. Normalmente no me gusta la comida española. Cuando voy a Málaga, hablo inglés, pero en Madrid hablé español. En Málaga me alojo en un camping, sin embargo, en Madrid me alojé en un hotel de cinco estrellas.

**2**  **Look back at Activity 1 and complete the table.**

| Normally | Last year |
|---|---|
| *Ejemplo: goes to Málaga* | |
| | |
| | |
| | |
| | |

**3**  **Write about your own holidays.**

Normalmente …                    pero el año pasado …

_____

_____

_____

_____

_____

_____

**1** Put these expressions into the correct column and add the English.

| Me gustó | ¡Qué ...! | Fue ... | _____é |
|---|---|---|---|
| *Ejemplo:* *me gustó = I liked it (it pleased me)* | | | |

| | | | |
|---|---|---|---|
| me encantó | disfruté | ¡qué desastre! | no me gustó |
| fue emocionante | fue increíble | ¡qué aburrido! | fue regular |
| lo pasé muy mal | lo pasé bomba | | |

**2** Colour the positive opinions in red. Colour the negative opinions in green.

**3** Read this text aloud, adding an opinion in Spanish each time you see ☺ or ☹.

> Fui de vacaciones a Cuba ☺. Me alojé en un hotel de lujo ☺. Fui con mi hermano y mis padres ☹. Fuimos a la playa ☺. Bailamos en una discoteca ☺. Viajamos nueve horas en avión ☹.

**4** Write about your own holiday in Spain, giving details of what you liked and what you didn't.

_____

_____

_____

_____

**1** **Roll a dice to see what you are going to buy and for whom.**

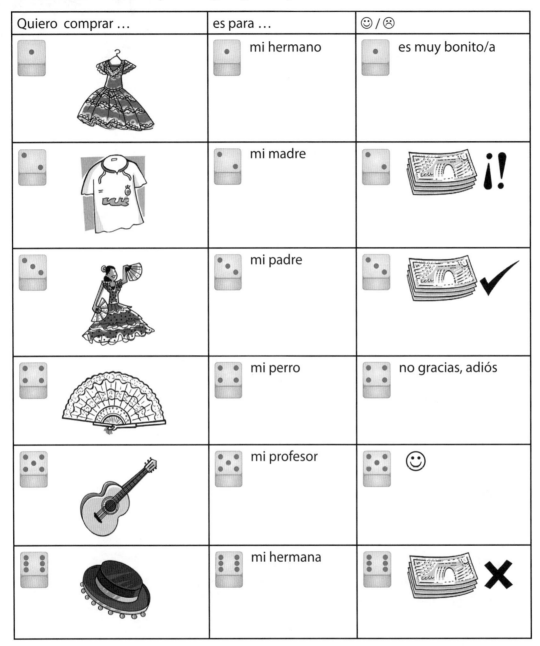

| Quiero comprar … | es para … | ☺ / ☹ |
|---|---|---|
| | mi hermano | es muy bonito/a |
| | mi madre | ¡! |
| | mi padre | ✔ |
| | mi perro | no gracias, adiós |
| | mi profesor | ☺ |
| | mi hermana | ✘ |

**2** 🎧 **Listen to the questions and use your answers from Activity 1 to take part in the conversation.**

**3** **Repeat Activities 1 and 2 until you get to 'no gracias, adiós'.**

**4** **Write out one of your conversations, complete with the shopkeeper's part.**

**Recuerdo**

The preterite tense is used to say what happened in the past.

**1** Draw lines to match each verb with its infinitive. You must not cross any lines once you have drawn them!

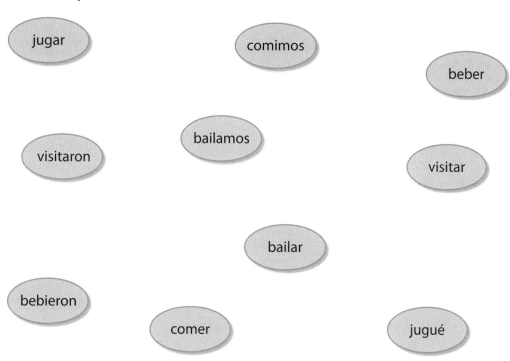

jugar

comimos

beber

bailamos

visitaron

visitar

bailar

bebieron

comer

jugué

**2** Find the Spanish for the following.

**a** I played _____

**b** We danced _____

**c** They visited _____

**d** We ate _____

**e** They drank _____

**3** Put these sentences into the past tense.

**a** Tomar el sol en la playa (*We* …) _____

**b** Comer en un restaurante (*She* …) _____

**c** Nadar en el mar (*They* …) _____

**d** Viajar en avión (*I* …) _____

**1** **Colour in these sentences. Use blue for past, green for present and red for future.**

    **a** Fui de vacaciones a España el año pasado.

    **b** Voy a ir de vacaciones a Francia el próximo año.

    **c** Normalmente voy de vacaciones a Grecia.

    **d** Mañana voy a visitar un castillo.

    **e** Ayer fui a la playa.

    **f** Saqué fotos en la ciudad.

    **g** Voy a volver el próximo año.

    **h** Hace tres años fui al Caribe.

    **i** Un día voy a ir a Estados Unidos.

    **j** Nadé en la piscina.

**2** **Write these sentences with the first person verb in the correct time frame: past, or future.**

    **a** El año pasado (tomar) el sol en la playa _____

    **b** Mañana (ir) a la playa _____

    **c** Ayer (comer) en un restaurante _____

    **d** El próximo martes (visitar) un museo _____

**3** **Write a postcard home. Include three things you did yesterday and three things you are going to do tomorrow.**

## ¿Qué se puede hacer? — **What can you do?**

| | |
|---|---|
| se puede | *you can / you are allowed* |
| no se puede | *you can't / you are not allowed* |
| se puede visitar | *you can visit* |
| se puede ir | *you can go* |
| se puede ver | *you can see* |
| se puede pasear | *you can go for a walk* |
| se puede pescar | *you can fish* |
| se puede comprar | *you can shop / buy* |
| se puede jugar | *you can play* |
| se puede hacer | *you can do* |
| el río | *the river* |
| al aire libre | *outdoors / outside* |
| lamentablemente | *unfortunately* |

## ¿Adónde fuiste? — **Where did you go?**

| | |
|---|---|
| el verano pasado | *last summer* |
| el invierno pasado | *last winter* |
| el año pasado | *last year* |
| hace dos años | *two years ago* |
| el pasado junio | *last June* |
| las Navidades pasadas | *last Christmas* |
| hizo sol | *it was sunny* |
| hizo calor | *it was hot* |
| hizo frío | *it was cold* |
| hizo viento | *it was windy* |
| hizo buen tiempo | *the weather was nice* |
| hizo mal tiempo | *the weather was bad* |
| estuvo nublado | *it was cloudy* |
| hubo tormenta | *there was a storm* |
| hubo niebla | *it was foggy* |
| llovió | *it rained* |

## ¿Qué hiciste? — **What did you do?**

| | |
|---|---|
| alojarse / nos alojamos | *to stay / we stayed (accommodation)* |
| hacer / hice vela | *to do / I did sailing* |
| tomar / tomé el sol | *to sunbathe / I sunbathed* |
| bañarse / me bañé en el mar | *to swim / I swam in the sea* |
| comer / comimos comida típica | *to eat / we ate typical food* |
| relajarse / nos relajamos | *to relax / we relaxed* |
| pasear / paseamos | *to go for a walk / we went for a walk* |
| sacar / saqué muchas fotos | *to take / I took lots of photos* |
| salir / salí de compras | *to go out / I went out shopping* |
| comprar / compré recuerdos | *to buy / I bought souvenirs* |
| escribir / escribí unas postales | *to write / I wrote some postcards* |
| la mayoría de las tardes | *most evenings* |
| volver / volví a casa | *to return / I returned home* |

## ¿Lo pasaste bien? — **Did you have a good time?**

| | |
|---|---|
| ¡Lo pasé / pasamos fenomenal! | *I / we had a great time!* |
| ¡Lo pasé / pasamos bomba! | *I / we had a blast!* |

| | |
|---|---|
| ¡Qué aburrido! | *How boring!* |
| ¡Qué desastre! | *What a disaster!* |
| fue / fueron regular | *it was / they were average* |
| fue / fueron muy emocionante(s) | *it was / they were very exciting* |
| fue / fueron increíble(s) | *it was / they were incredible* |
| no estuvo / estuvieron mal | *it wasn't / they weren't bad* |
| me / nos encantó | *I / we loved it* |
| me / nos gustó | *I / we liked it* |

## ¿Qué compraste? — **What did you buy?**

| | |
|---|---|
| un imán | *a magnet* |
| unas castañuelas | *castanets* |
| un abanico | *a (typically Spanish) fan* |
| una camiseta | *a t-shirt* |
| un vestido de flamenco | *a flamenco dress* |
| una guitarra española | *a Spanish guitar* |
| una muñeca | *a doll* |
| un sombrero | *a hat* |
| un llavero | *a key ring* |
| unas gafas de sol | *sunglasses* |
| el/la dependiente | *shop assistant* |
| el/la cliente | *customer* |
| ¿Qué deseas? | *What would you like?* |
| ¿Cuánto cuesta? | *How much does it cost?* |
| muy caro/a | *very expensive* |
| algo más barato/a | *something cheaper* |
| ¡Mira! | *Look!* |
| Me lo quedo | *I'll take it* |
| ¿Algo más? | *Anything else?* |

## Checklist

| How well do you think you can do the following? | | | |
|---|---|---|---|
| Write a sentence for each one if you can. | | | |
| | **I can do this well** | **I can do this but not very well** | **I can't do this yet** |
| 1. Say what you can do in town | | | |
| 2. Talk about the weather in the past | | | |
| 3. Say what you did on holiday | | | |
| 4. Use the preterite tense | | | |
| 5. Use time markers | | | |

**1** Read the texts and write the correct name under each bar chart.

> Navego por internet de vez en cuando, pero no participo nunca en los chats. Prefiero hablar por teléfono o utilizar correo electrónico. Veo la televisión todos los días, sobre todo los documentales. *David*

> Me encanta ver la televisión. Todos los días veo telenovelas. Me encantan. No tengo ordenador, y no navego nunca por internet. De vez en cuando me gusta escuchar música en la radio, y a menudo leo revistas. *Ana*

> Veo la televisión, pero no mucho. Prefiero jugar con videojuegos. Juego todos los días en internet. Tengo amigos en Australia, Estados Unidos, Inglaterra. Jugamos y a veces chateamos. *Felipe*

> Una vez a la semana compro una revista sobre música y la leo. También me gusta navegar por internet a menudo y escuchar música en la radio. No veo nunca la televisión. *Ofelia*

**a**

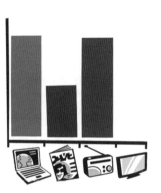

_____

**b**

_____

**c**

_____

**d**

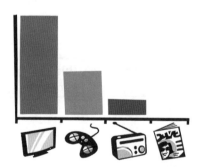

_____

**e**

_____

**2** Write a similar text for the bar chart which is left.

_____

_____

_____

# 4B.2 El cine y los libros

**1** **Missing vowels! Write out these types of film in full.**

*Ejemplo:*

**a** n plcl rmntc – *una película romántica*

**b** n plcl d trrr _____

**c** n plcl d cnc-fccn _____

**d** n plcl d vqrs _____

**e** n plcl d ccn _____

**f** n plcl d mstr _____

**g** n plcl d grr _____

**h** n cmd _____

**2** **Talk about whether you like each type of film.**

*Ejemplo:*

> Me encantan las películas románticas
> porque son emocionantes.

| | | |
|---|---|---|
| me encantan | | no me gustan mucho |
| | me gustan | |
| | prefiero | divertidas |
| odio | | |
| | | tontas | graciosas |
| no me gustan | emocionantes | |

**3** 🎧 **Listen to Alvina and think of a film you would recommend she sees.**

_____

**1** 🎧 **Read the film titles. Listen – who saw which film? Write the correct letter.**

**a** Agente Azul y la bomba nuclear

**b** En tren para Tombuctú

**c** La luna llena: sangre a medianoche

**d** Romeo y Julieta

**e** Batalla contra el Imperio

**1** ☐

**2** ☐

**3** ☐

**4** ☐

**5** ☐

**2** **Translate into English.**

Vi una película romántica de ciencia-ficción. Era una comedia. Un astronauta se enamoró de una estudiante. El novio de la estudiante, que era vampiro, robó una bomba nuclear. El astronauta solucionó el problema cuando descubrió un nuevo planeta.

_____

_____

_____

_____

_____

**1** 🎧 **Read through the questions. Listen.**
**Which question is each person answering?**

1 _____   4 _____

2 _____   5 _____

3 _____   6 _____

**A  Información personal**
i   ¿Cómo te llamas?
ii  ¿Cuántos años tienes?
iii ¿Cómo eres?

**B  Tu vida**
i   ¿Qué te gusta hacer en tu tiempo libre?
ii  ¿Cómo es tu rutina diaria?
iii ¿Dónde vives?

**C  Tus vacaciones**
i   ¿Adónde vas de vacaciones?
ii  ¿Qué haces cuando estás de vacaciones?
iii ¿Qué hiciste durante las vacaciones del año pasado?

**D  Los medios**
i   ¿Cómo te comunicas con tus amigos – por móvil, correo electrónico, SMS?
ii  ¿Qué te gusta ver en la televisión?
iii ¿Cuál fue la última película que viste? ¿De qué trató?

**2**  **Interview yourself in Spanish using the questions above.**

**1** 🎧 **Listen and follow the three sentences on the grid.**
**Sensible (S) or nonsense (N)?**

**1** S / N

**2** S / N

**3** S / N

| | | | |
|---|---|---|---|
| Me encanta | ver | una revista | porque es divertido. |
| Me gusta | leer | los deberes | porque es aburrido. |
| No me gusta | hacer | la televisión | porque es emocionante. |
| Prefiero | hablar con | la radio | porque es educativo. |
| Odio | escuchar | una hamburguesa | porque es fácil. |
| Me gustaría | comer | mis amigos | porque es tonto. |

**2** **Roll a dice and write out the sentences you make. Sensible or nonsense?**

_____

_____

_____

**3** **Use the grid to keep talking for one minute.**

| y | pero | porque | por ejemplo |

**Recuerdo**

To say 'I like it' in Spanish you say 'It pleases me': *Me gusta.*

**1** **Think like a Spanish person. Complete the grids.**

*Ejemplo:*

| English | I like it |
|---|---|
| Inbetweenish | It pleases me |
| Spanish | Me gusta |

| English | Do you like it? |
|---|---|
| Inbetweenish | |
| Spanish | |

| English | |
|---|---|
| Inbetweenish | |
| Spanish | Me gustan |

| English | We like it |
|---|---|
| Inbetweenish | |
| Spanish | |

| English | |
|---|---|
| Inbetweenish | |
| Spanish | Le gusta |

| English | I liked it |
|---|---|
| Inbetweenish | |
| Spanish | Me gustó |

**2** **Translate into Spanish.**

**a** I like to watch TV.

_____

**b** Do you like music?

_____

**c** He likes to watch TV.

_____

**d** She likes to talk on the phone.

_____

**e** I like films.

_____

**f** I liked the film.

_____

**g** We like to go to the cinema.

_____

**1** Complete the grid.

| Verb | Infinitive | Ending | Meaning |
|---|---|---|---|
| come | *Ejemplo: comer* | *present – he/she/it* | *he eats* |
| bebí | | | |
| habla | | | |
| jugué | | | |
| fuimos | | | |
| escucho | | | |

**2** Use a dictionary to find the meaning of these verbs.

salvamos       secuestró       perdieron

_____    _____    _____

rescatan       se casan

_____    _____

**3** Work out what the underlined verbs mean.
Then translate the whole text into English.

En la película un gato mágico <u>ayuda</u> a una niña. <u>Buscan</u> a sus padres. <u>Viajan</u> por todo el mundo. <u>Cumplen</u> una serie de aventuras peligrosas. Se <u>reúnen</u> con sus padres.

_____

_____

_____

_____

_____

## Los medios y la televisión — *The media and television*

| | |
|---|---|
| hablo por teléfono | *I talk on the phone* |
| navego por internet | *I surf the net* |
| veo la televisión | *I watch TV* |
| escucho la radio | *I listen to the radio* |
| juego con videojuegos | *I play computer games* |
| utilizo el correo electrónico | *I email* |
| leo los periódicos | *I read the newspapers* |
| leo revistas | *I read magazines* |
| participo en los chats | *I use chatrooms* |
| de vez en cuando | *sometimes* |
| todos los días | *every day* |
| una vez / tres veces a la semana | *once / three times a week* |
| nunca / a menudo | *never / often* |
| divertido/a | *entertaining* |
| gracioso/a / tonto/a | *funny / stupid* |
| emocionante | *exciting* |
| informativo/a | *informative* |
| las noticias | *news* |
| las series | *series* |
| las telenovelas | *TV soaps* |
| los anuncios | *adverts* |
| los concursos | *game shows* |
| los dibujos animados | *cartoons* |
| los documentales | *documentaries* |
| los programas deportivos | *sports programmes* |
| los programas musicales | *music programmes* |

## El cine y los libros — *Cinema and books*

| | |
|---|---|
| una película romántica | *a romantic film* |
| una película de terror | *a horror film* |
| una película de ciencia-ficción | *a sci-fi film* |
| una película de vaqueros | *a cowboy film* |
| una película de acción | *an action film* |
| una película de misterio | *a mystery film* |
| una película de guerra | *a war film* |
| una comedia | *a comedy* |
| la fantasía | *fantasy* |

## ¿De qué trató? ¿Qué pasó? — *What was it about? What happened?*

| | |
|---|---|
| un asesinato | *a murder* |
| un atentado | *a terrorist attack* |
| un robo | *a robbery* |
| un secuestro | *a kidnap* |
| un timo | *a scam* |
| un viaje | *a journey* |
| una amistad | *a friendship* |
| una guerra | *a war* |
| una historia de amor | *a love story* |
| una lucha entre el bien y el mal | *a struggle between good and evil* |
| una misión secreta | *a secret mission* |
| vampiros | *vampires* |

| | |
|---|---|
| buscar | *to look for* |
| batallar | *to fight* |
| robar | *to rob* |
| descubrir | *to find* |
| solucionar | *to solve* |
| enamorarse de | *to fall in love with* |

## En mi opinión … — *In my opinion …*

| | |
|---|---|
| es muy … | *it's very …* |
| puede ser … | *it can be …* |
| útil / rápido/a | *useful / quick* |
| personal | *personal* |
| educativo/a | *educational* |
| entretenido/a | *entertaining* |
| fácil / peligroso/a | *easy / dangerous* |
| una ventaja es … | *an advantage is …* |
| una desventaja es … | *a disadvantage is …* |
| lo malo / bueno es que … | *the bad / good thing is …* |
| es una pérdida de tiempo | *it's a waste of time* |
| se puede hacer … | *you can do it …* |
| con amigos / solo / en casa / donde quieras | *with friends / alone / at home / wherever you like* |
| se puede llevar consigo / adonde quieras | *you can take it with you / wherever you like* |
| (no) necesitas tecnología especial | *you (don't) need special technology* |
| (no) es caro/a | *it's (not) expensive* |

## Extra — *Extra*

| | |
|---|---|
| una tontería | *a stupid thing* |
| tienes que verlo | *you have to see it* |
| ¿No conoces …? | *Don't you know …?* |

# Checklist

| How well do you think you can do the following? | | | |
|---|---|---|---|
| Write a sentence for each one if you can. | | | |
| | I can do this well | I can do this but not very well | I can't do this yet |
| 1. Talk about types of films and TV programmes | | | |
| 2. Talk about how you communicate with your friends | | | |
| 3. Say what happened in a film | | | |
| 4. Give opinions | | | |
| 5. Look up verbs in a dictionary | | | |

# Zoom in on your students' needs for KS3 Spanish
## with fully integrated video drama

**Zoom español** is an inspiring two-part Spanish course offering fresh, exciting material and a fully integrated video drama for the whole ability range at Key Stage 3.

The course is flexible and relevant, taking account of the ever increasing diversity of students' abilities and language learning backgrounds. It is fully up-to-date and follows the renewed Key Stage 3 Framework for Languages and the revised Key Stage 3 Programme of Study.

This Workbook provides:

- differentiated practice material for the key language in each unit
- consolidation of key grammar points and language learning skills
- checklists and vocabulary lists for each unit so students can revise the language they've learnt and check their progress
- extra audio material for listening practice

| | |
|---|---|
| Zoom español Student Book 1 | 978 0 19 912754 2 |
| Zoom español Foundation Workbook 1 | 978 0 19 912814 3 |
| Zoom español Higher Workbook 1 | 978 0 19 912815 0 |
| Zoom español Teacher Book 1 | 978 0 19 912758 0 |
| Zoom español Audio CDs 1 | 978 0 19 912757 3 |
| Zoom español Interactive Oxbox 1 | 978 0 19 912760 3 |
| Zoom español Assessment Oxbox 1 | 978 0 19 912761 0 |

## OXFORD
UNIVERSITY PRESS

**How to get in touch:**
**web** www.oxfordsecondary.co.uk
**email** schools.enquiries.uk@oup.com
**tel** 01536 452620
**fax** 01865 313472

ISBN 978-0-19-912756-6